Malcolm Galloway and Kalyan Chatakondu

The MUSIC BRIDGE

An Electronic Keyboard Course For All

The
MUSIC
BRIDGE

Typeset in Agenda

Editing, design, typesetting and publishing by UK Book Publishing

www.ukbookpublishing.com

ISBN: 978-1-914195-93-8

If you play the electronic keyboard
The Music Bridge is the course that will help you progress more
quickly and allow you to explore the world of music at
your leisure.

This "mini-course" is super easy and can be enjoyed on its own or as a supplement to other music material

---

♩ Some well-known "classical" and "traditional" pieces are included that young and old alike will want to play again and again.

♩ Each piece introduces an important skill or technique.

♩ Words have been included to help you follow the music more easily.

♩ Fun facts about the individual composers of the pieces will help you connect with the music more readily.

♩ This course has been created by Malcolm Galloway, an experienced professional keyboard player and qualified music teacher for over 20 years.

THE MUSIC

1. MUSETTE — Johann Sebastian Bach

2. BAGATELLE FOR FRIENDS — Ludwig van Beethoven

3. JOYFUL SOUNDS — Ludwig van Beethoven

4. TRUMPET VOLUNTARY — Jeremiah Clarke

5. ARIETTA — Muzio Clementi

6. SERENADE — Stephen Foster

7. HAPPINESS — George Frideric Handel

8. JAZZ IN THE AIR — George Frideric Handel

9. MARCH — George Frideric Handel

10. PASTORAL SCENE — George Frideric Handel

11. ROYAL MINUET — George Frideric Handel

12. ADAGIO — Wolfgang Amadeus Mozart

13. ANDANTE — Wolfgang Amadeus Mozart

14. HUMMING SONG — Robert Schumann

15. AUTUMN — Antonio Vivaldi

16. C TO A AND WE'RE AWAY — Traditional

17. LAVENDER'S BLUE — Traditional

18. MICHAEL ROW THE BOAT — Traditional

19. TWINKLE, TWINKLE LITTLE STAR — Traditional

20. WHEN THE SAINTS GO MARCHING IN — Traditional

INDEX A – TEACHING POINTS

THE LEFT HAND

The left hand plays the accompaniments to each melody.

Only chords C, F, G and A minor (Am) are used.

Note C as shown on the keyboard is an octave below middle C.

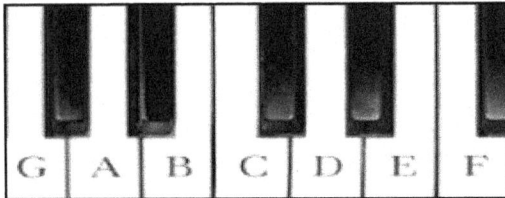

The Keyboard

C Chord

G			C		E	
5			2		1	

F Chord

	A		C			F
	4		2			1

G Chord

G		B		D		
5		3		1		

Am Chord

	A		C		E	
	4		2		1	

THE CHORDS

Single-Finger Chords
Using the single fingered chord facility, press note C for C chord, F for F chord and G for G Chord. See your keyboard manual to produce minor chords in other ways

Fingered Chords
This method of producing chords requires the left hand to play all the three notes of a chord at the same time. In the diagram opposite, the finger numbers are shown for each note to be played

Percussive Accompaniment
The suggested styles are optional, but fun to use!

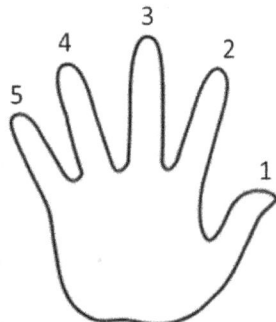

4

THE RIGHT HAND

The melodies are played by the right hand

Only two hand positions are used

The first is with the first finger (the thumb) on middle C

The second is with the first finger on D (the note to the right of middle C)

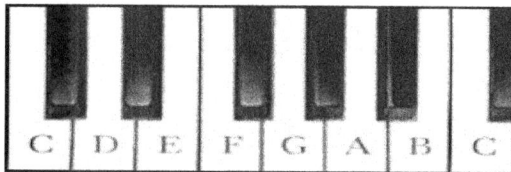

The Keyboard

The hand positions

all pieces begin in the first-hand position except pieces 11,18 and 20 which begin in the second-hand position

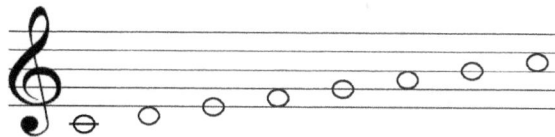

The pitch of each note as shown on the stave

Middle C D E F G A B C

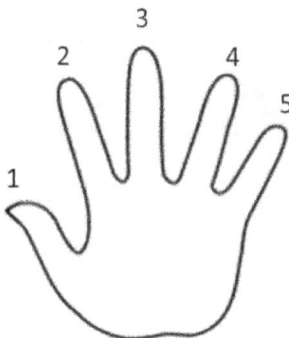

Finger Numbers
Finger numbers are shown under each note to be played. When the hand needs to move to a new position (up or down one white note), a hyphen between the two adjacent finger numbers is shown.

THE
MUSIC

"My music is elaborate, picturesque and passionate. I enjoy playing the harpsichord as well as playing the pipe organ."

"I have written so much music that some people don't believe I've had the time to write it all!"

"I've specialised in composing sacred music suitable for performance in a church rather than in the theatre."

"When I was a young boy, I went to live with my elder brother. I copied much of his music when he was asleep!"

JOHANN SEBASTIAN BACH

1. MUSETTE

Johann Sebastian Bach

INFO
One right-hand postion
Chords: C, F and G
Voice: Harpshichord
Style: Ballad
Tempo:126

"I often quarrel with my friends. Once when I was playing the piano, I was so annoyed with them that I hit the keys so hard that the strings snapped!"

"I moved to Vienna in Austria in 1792 where I spent most of my time composing rather than playing music."

"I wrote four overtures for my opera, Fidelio, between 1805 and 1814. The first three are known as the Leonora Overtures as the opera was originally called Leonora."

"Joyful Sounds, originally called Ode to Joy, is my most popular tune."

LUDWIG VAN BEETHOVEN

2. BAGATELLE FOR FRIENDS

Ludwig van Beethoven

Some folks I know are kind and help - ful.

"Saints" I think to you and me.

Good to have friends a - round,

al - ways there for when we

need their com - pa - ny.

INFO
Two right-hand positions
Chords: C, F and G
Voice: Piano
Style: 16 Beat
Tempo: 112

"I fell in love with a woman called Antonia Brentano, but she never got my letter telling her that I loved her."

"I like jokes. I transformed the graceful minuet into a scherzo in my symphonies." (scherzo is the Italian word for a joke!)

"My music is very emotional and rather dramatic. I've composed 26 bagatelles for my friends to play."

"I was born in Bonn in Germany in 1770. I did not have a happy childhood as my father regularly got drunk."

LUDWIG VAN BEETHOVEN

3. JOYFUL SOUNDS

Ludwig van Beethoven

C   G

3   3   4   5   5   4   3   2
Sing   to   all   who   care   to   list – en,

C   G

1   1   2   3   3   2   1   2
sing   some   joy – ful   songs   we   know.

C   G

3   3   4   5   5   4   3   2
Sing   to   all   who   care   to   list – en,

Am   F   G   C

1   2   3   2   2   1   1
sing   songs   that   make   our   hearts   glow.

INFO
One right-hand position
Chords: C, F, G and Am
Voice: Vocal Ensemble
Style: 8 Beat
Tempo: 116

"I was born in London in 1673 and sang in a choir before becoming an organist and composer."

"I once loved a beautiful woman who was of superior rank, so I could not marry her."

"I enjoy playing the church organ and was, for a while, the organist at St Paul's Cathedral in London."

"My music is considered to be 'theatrical' and very appealing!"

JEREMIAH CLARKE

4. TRUMPET VOLUNTARY

Jeremiah Clarke

Play - the - trum - pet loud and

clear for all to hear.

Let - our - fears and wor - ries

sim - ply dis - ap - pear.

INFO

One right hand position
Chords: C, F, G and Am
Voice: Trumpet
Style: Country
Tempo: 120

𝅝 Hold this note (a semibreve) for four beats

"I was born in Italy in 1752, and was educated in England."

"My main interest in life is playing the piano."

"Many people, including Beethoven, enjoy playing my piano music."

"In 1812, I established in London my own piano manufacturing business called 'Clementi and Co'."

MUZIO CLEMENTI

5. ARIETTA

Muzio Clementi

INFO

An arietta is a short operatic song.
Two right hand positions
Chords: C, F and G
Voice: Piano
Style: Swing
Tempo: 100
Phrasing (Lift the right hand off the keyboard after a comma and full stop)

"In 1846, I was employed by my brother as a bookkeeper."

"I became America's first professional songwriter, earning two cents for each copy of my music sold."

"I am a shy person. I often use the name of another person rather than my own on my music."

"My song, Oh Susanna, is one of the most popular songs of all time. Susanna is the name of my sister and because of this song, she is now more famous than me!"

STEPHEN FOSTER

6. SERENADE

Stephen Foster

3   5 - 4   5   4   2 - 1   2
come   from   Al - a - bam - a   with   my

3   3   2   1   2   1   2   3   5 - 4   5
ban - jo   on   my   knee.   -   Hope   to   se - re - nade   my

4   2 - 1   2   3   3   2   2   1
true   love   in   the   hope   she'll   mar - ry   me.

INFO
Two right-hand positions
Chords: C, F and G
Voice: Banjo
Style: Swing
Tempo: 168
The first two notes of the piece are called 'pick up' notes and in this case are played 'staccato' ie each note is played
sharply detached and separately from each other

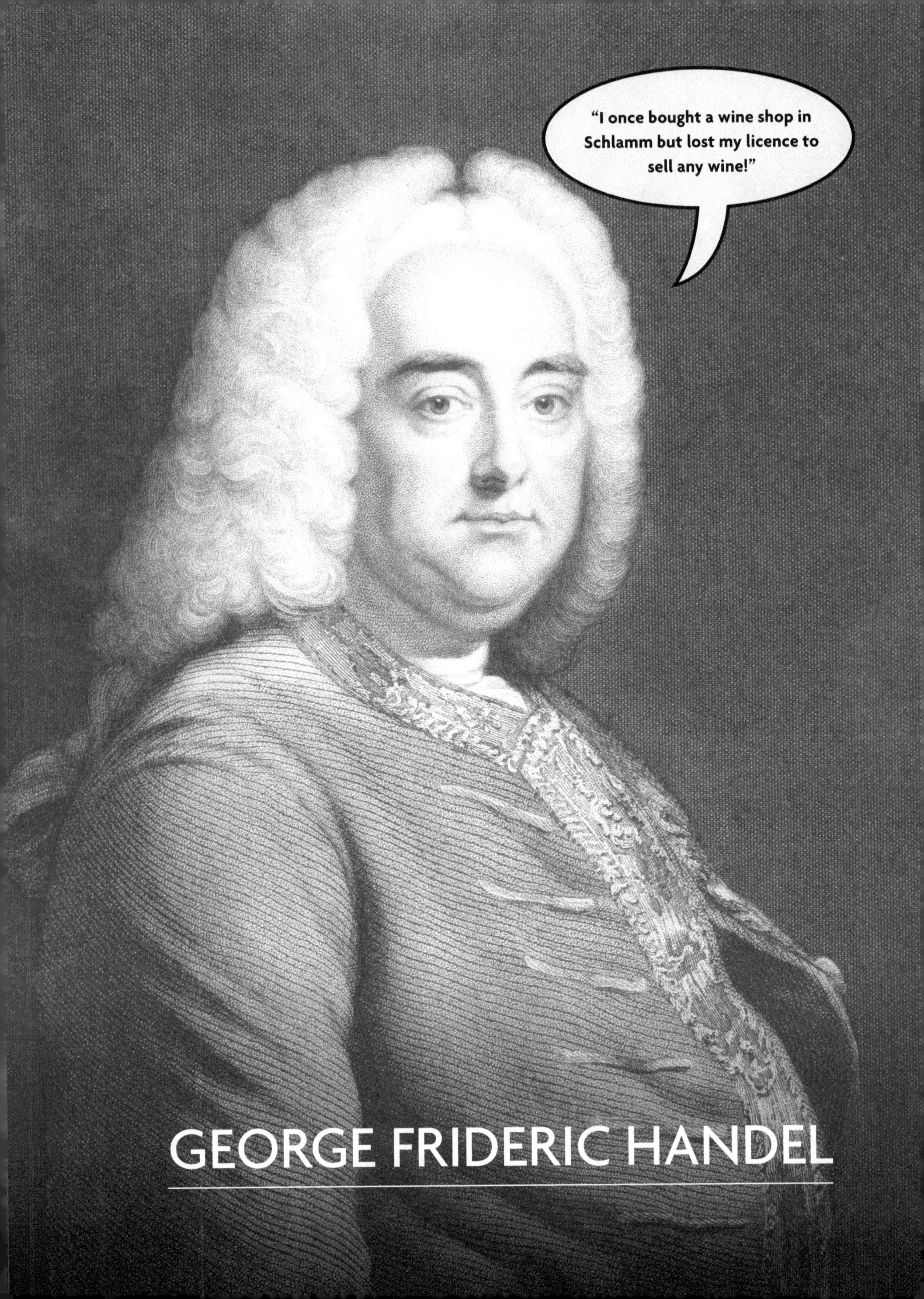

GEORGE FRIDERIC HANDEL

7. HAPPINESS

George Frideric Handel

C

3 2 1 2 2 3 2 1 2
We are smi – ling be - cause we're hap - py,

F   **G**

3 4 4 3 4 5
hap – py as we can be.

C   **C**

3 2 1 2 2 3 2 1 2 2
We are smi – ling be - cause we're hap - py, be

C   **G**   **C**

3 3 2 3 2 1
hap – py like - me.

INFO

This piece, composed in 1735, is a minuet from Handel's opera, 'Alcina'

One right hand position

Chords: C and G

Voice: Piccolo

Style: Waltz

Tempo 116

Play these three notes in the space of one crotchet beat

"I wrote the music for the Royal Fireworks in 1749. The fireworks were disappointing as they just fizzled out, but the music is still popular today!"

"The Hallelujah Chorus in my oratorio, 'Messiah', is my most popular piece. When King George II heard it, he rose to his feet, and audiences to this day also stand for it."

GEORGE FRIDERIC HANDEL

8. JAZZ IN THE AIR

George Frideric Handel

3	5	1	3	2		3	5	1	3	2
Try	and	swing	this	tune.		This	is	what	you	do.

5	4	4	2	3	4	2	1
Change	the	rhy – thm	of	the	qua	–	vers.

INFO
One right-hand position
Chords: C F G and Am
Voice: String Ensemble
Style: Ballad
Tempo: 76

Play the pairs of quavers (♫) like this (♩♪)

"I enjoy the 'free and easy' lifestyle of London and I regard England as my own country."

GEORGE FRIDERIC HANDEL

9. MARCH

George Frideric Handel

Line 1 (C / C / G): Play the pipe and drum and dance, dance.
1 2 3 4 3 2 1 2

Line 2 (C / C / G): Play the pipe and drum this way.
3 2 3 4 5 4 3 4 3 2

Line 3 (C / C / TO CODA): Bang on the drum, let us bang on the drum and
1 1 1 1 5 3 1 1 1 1 2

Line 4 (C / G / C / DC al CODA): dance to the tunes we play.
3 1 1 2 1 1

CODA (C / F / G): dance to the tunes we play Hip, hip, hoo - ray!
3 3 4 5 4 3 2 3

INFO
One right-hand position
Chords: C, F and G
Voice: String Ensemble
Style: 16 Beat
Tempo:120

D.C. al CODA (Repeat the piece from the beginning until the end of line 3, then play the CODA)

"As a boy I used to secretly play the clavichord when my family was asleep."

"I once had a duel with another composer called Johann Mattheson. Luckily his sword hit a button on my jacket or he might have killed me!"

GEORGE FRIDERIC HANDEL

10. PASTORAL SCENE

George Frideric Handel

INFO
Two right-hand positions
Chords: C, F and G
Voice: String Ensemble
Style: Waltz
Tempo: 108
Play the melody smoothly (legato) with no breaks in sound between the notes.

"Queen Anne liked my music and employed me when I moved to London in 1712."

"I was born in Halle in Germany in 1685. My father was a lawyer who did not think I should follow a musical career."

GEORGE FRIDERIC HANDEL

11. ROYAL MINUET

George Frideric Handel

C ... G C ... C ... G ... C

1 1 2 3 ... 2 1 ... 1 ... 1 2 1 ... 2 ... 2 3 2 2 ... 3 3 4 ... 3

In Green Park Lon-don, ... fans of Han-del ... came from a-far to ... hear his mu - sic

G ... C ... F ... G ... C

2 ... 2 3 4 ... 4 ... 5 4 3 ... 2 ... 1 2 3 - 4 ... 5 4 ... 3 ... 2

played. ... Hunt-ing horns were ... play ing loud - ly, ... ket-tle drums were ... dis played proud - ly.

Am ... G ... C F G ... C

1 2 1 ... 1 ... 4 ... 2 ... 3 ... 3 4 3 2 ... 1 ... 1

Stur - dy tunes like ... this one the ... peo - ple came ... to ... hear.

INFO
Two right-hand positions
Chords: C, F, G and Am
Voice: Trumpet
Style: Waltz
Tempo: 125

The first, the smaller, of these two notes is an acciaccatura, to be played on the beat as quickly as possible.

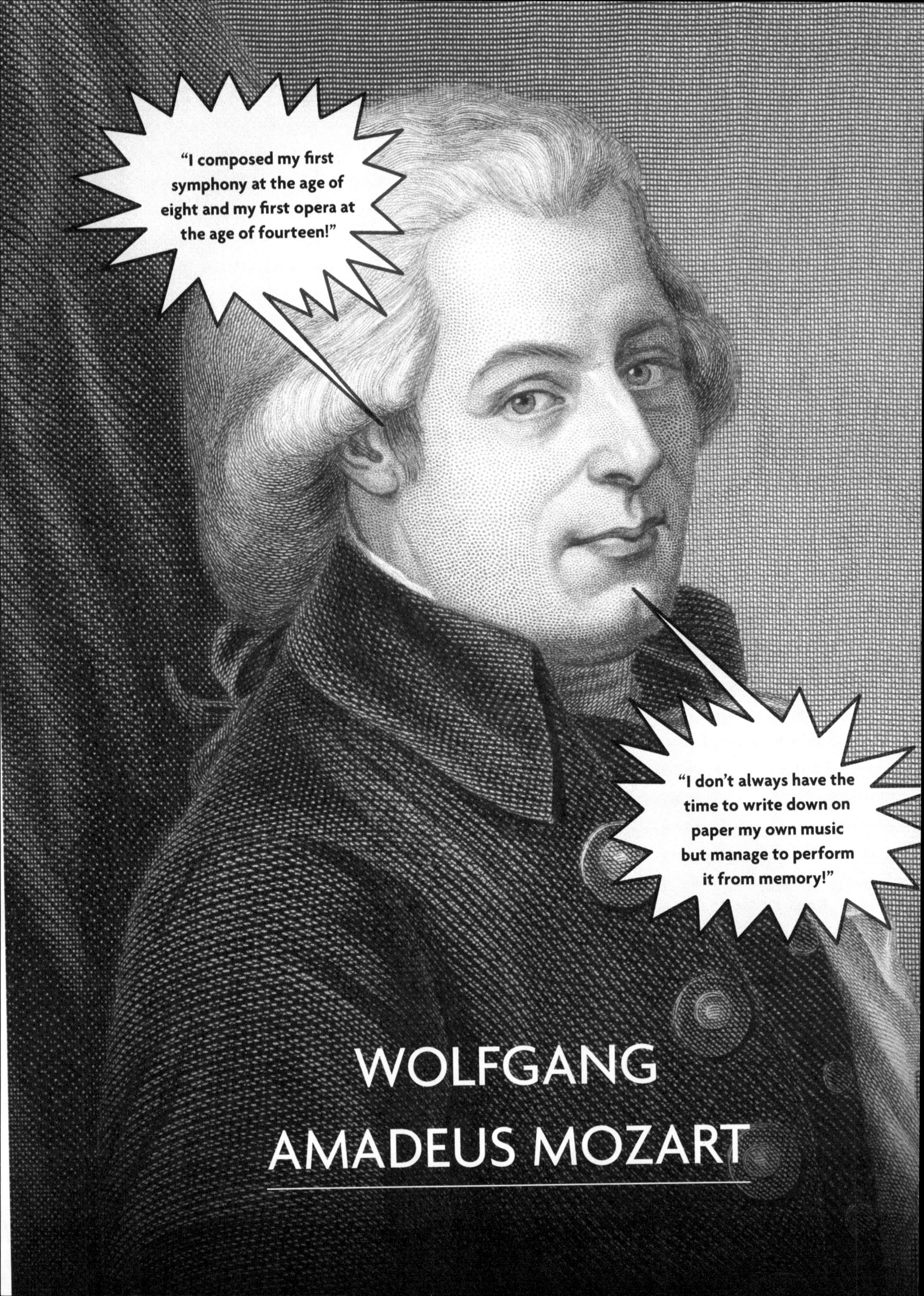

WOLFGANG AMADEUS MOZART

12. ADAGIO

Wolfgang Amadeus Mozart

Come Sep - tem - ber.

Time to see each - oth - er in the sun - shine.

Come De - cem - ber,

cold - er but it should be fine.

INFO
Two right-hand positions
Chords: C, F and G
Voice: String Ensemble
Style: Ballad
Tempo: 100

𝄽 is one crotchet beat rest

"I have a young English friend, violinist Thomas Linley, who lives in Bath in Somerset, England."

"I can play the piano with my eyes closed!"

WOLFGANG AMADEUS MOZART

13. ANDANTE

Wolfgang Amadeus Mozart

INFO

One right-hand position

Chords: C, F and G

Voice: String Ensemble

Style: Waltz

Tempo: 100

Sequences: There is a sequence in this piece. Bars 1 and 2 are repeated at bars 3 and 4, but at a lower pitch.
The same passage is repeated from bar 9

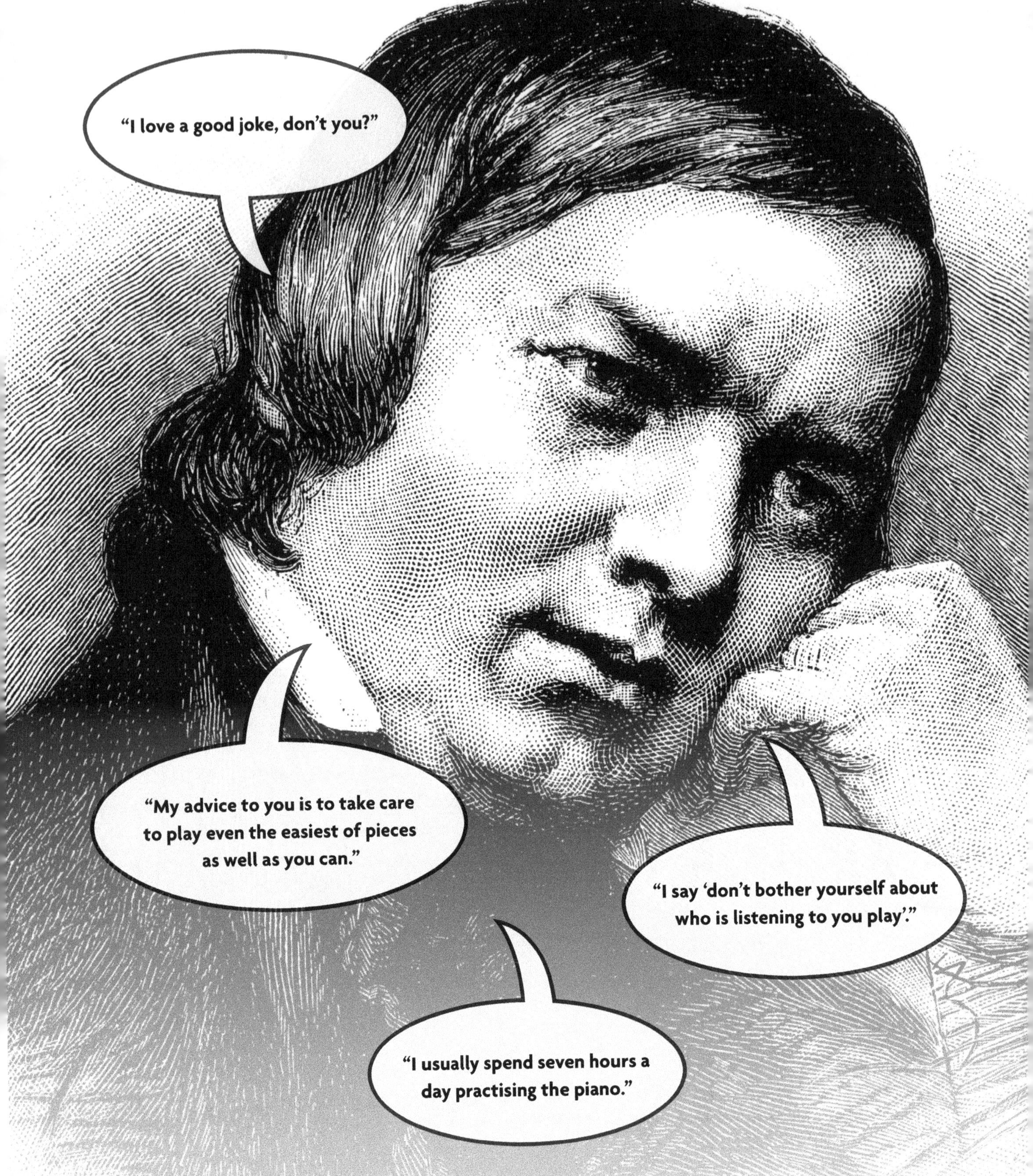

ROBERT SCHUMANN

14. HUMMING SONG

Robert Schumann

INFO

One right-hand position

Chords: C, F and G

Voice: Piano

Style: Ballad

Tempo: 104

pp (pianissimo): Reduce the volume to play the music very quietly

"I trained to be a priest for three years and was ordained at the age of 25. My nickname is 'Il Prete Rosso' ('The Red Priest') because I have red hair!"

"The style of my music is known as baroque. The composer Bach really likes my work. He is more famous than me!"

"I was born in Venice in 1678 the son of a Baker. I have written over 500 concertos and even some operas!"

"I have produced a large quantity of music including hundreds of concertos. You might say that I am a prolific composer!"

ANTONIO VIVALDI

15. AUTUMN

Antonio Vivaldi

INFO

One right-hand position

Chords: C and G

Voice: Piccolo

Style: Swing

Tempo: 190

The note E in the melody (played with the third finger) is played 25 times in this fast piece !

TRADITIONAL MELODIES
– English folk songs

16. C TO A AND WE'RE AWAY

Traditional

INFO
Two right-hand positions
Chords: C, F, G and Am
Voice: AltoSax
Style: 8 Beat
Tempo: 100

TRADITIONAL MELODIES
– English folk songs

17. LAVENDER'S BLUE

Traditional

C

1 5 5   5   4 3 2 1
La - ven - der's   blue, did - dle did - dle,

F   F

1 - 5 5   5   -
la - ven - der's green!

C   C

1 5 5   5   4 3 2 1
When I am king, did - dle did - dle,

G   C

4 3 4 3 2   1
you'll be - my queen.

INFO
Two right-hand positions
Chords: C, F and G
Voice: Clarinet
Style: Waltz
Tempo: 126

𝄆 𝄇 Play the music again between these two signs

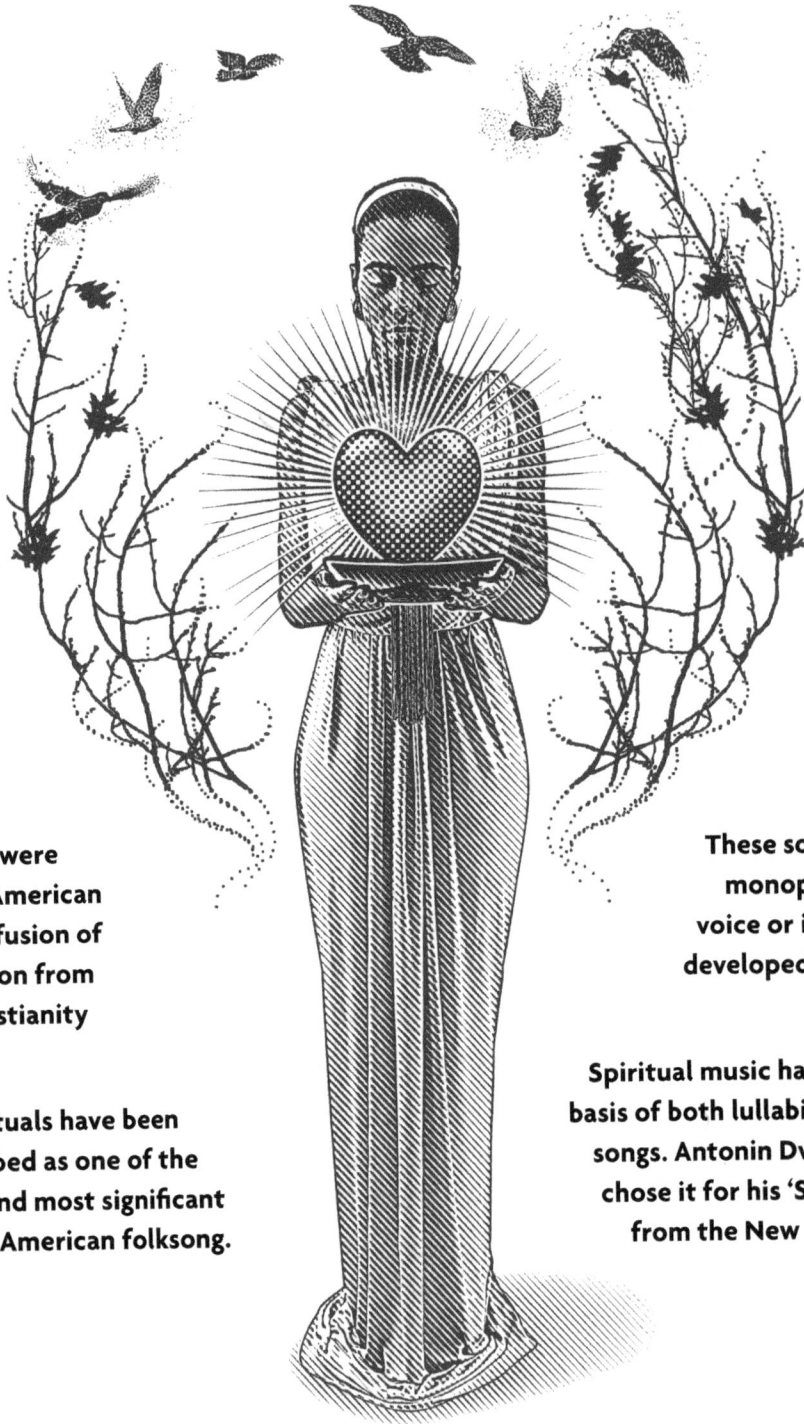

Their origins were usually African-American and represent a fusion of music and religion from Africa and Christianity

These songs were originally monophonic for a single voice or instrument but later developed into choral versions.

Spirituals have been described as one of the largest and most significant forms of American folksong.

Spiritual music has been the basis of both lullabies and work songs. Antonin Dvorak even chose it for his 'Symphony from the New World.'

TRADITIONAL MELODIES – 'SPIRITUALS'

18. MICHAEL ROW THE BOAT

Traditional

Lyrics: Mich - ael row the boat a - shore, hal - le - lu - yah. Mich - ael row the boat a - shore, hal - le - lu - yah.

INFO
Two right-hand positions
Chords: C, F, G and Am
Voice: Piano
Style: Swing
Tempo: 170

A lullaby or 'cradle song' is a soothing song usually sung to children at bedtime to 'lull' them to sleep but in some societies are used to pass down cultural tradition

Lullabies have a gentle rocking rhythm and classical music composers often wrote them for piano solo

The lyrics for 'Twinkle Twinkle Little Star' originated from a 19th century English poem by Jane Taylor, but it is sung to the tune of a French melody!

The full version of 'Twinkle Twinkle Little Star' has five verses and speaks of the wonder of stars lighting the way for travellers across the world

TRADITIONAL MELODIES – LULLABIES

19. TWINKLE, TWINKLE LITTLE STAR

Traditional

INFO

Two right-hand positions
Chords: C, F and G
Voice: Harp
Style: Ballad
Tempo: 126
D.C. al FINE (Repeat the first two lines of music)

'When the Saints Go Marching in' or simply known as 'The Saints' was famously recorded by Louis Armstrong in 1938

'The Saints' is an American gospel spiritual hymn that originated as a Christian hymn but is now often played by jazz bands!

The traditional lyrics of the 'Saints' are based on the Book of Revelation in the Bible

New Orleans style jazz songs in particular often had roots in Spirituals and Gospel Hymns

TRADITIONAL MELODIES – GOSPEL, JAZZ AND SPIRITUAL!

20. WHEN THE SAINTS GO MARCHING IN

Traditional

INFO
One right-hand position
Chords: C, F and G
Voice: Trumpet
Style: Swing
Tempo: 138

A tie is a curved line connecting two notes of the same pitch so extending the length of the first of the two notes

INDEX B – PERFORMANCE DETAILS

No.	MUSIC	VOICE NAME	STYLE NAME	TEMPO	HAND POSITIONS	CHORDS	BEATS PER BAR
1	Musette	Harpsichord	Ballad	126	One	C F G	4
2	Bagatelle for Friends	Piano	16 Beat	112	Two	C F G	4
3	Joyful Sounds	Vocal Ensemble	8 Beat	116	One	C F G Am	4
4	Trumpet Voluntary	Trumpet	Country	120	One	C F G Am	4
5	Arietta	Piano	Swing	100	Two	C F G	4
6	Serenade	Banjo	Swing	168	Two	C F G	4
7	Happiness	Piccolo	Waltz	116	One	C G	3
8	Jazz in the Air	String Ensemble	Ballad	76	One	C F G Am	4
9	March	String Ensemble	16 Beat	120	One	C F G	4
10	Pastoral Scene	String Ensemble	Waltz	108	Two	C F G	3
11	Royal Minuet	Trumpet	Waltz	125	Two	C F G Am	3
12	Adagio	String Ensemble	Ballad	100	Two	C F G	4
13	Andante	String Ensemble	Waltz	100	One	C F G	3
14	Humming Song	Piano	Ballad	104	One	C F G	4
15	Autumn	Piccolo	Swing	190	One	C G	4
16	C to A and We're Away	Alto Sax	8 Beat	100	Two	C F G Am	4
17	Lavender's Blue	Clarinet	Waltz	126	Two	C F G	3
18	Michael Row the Boat	Piano	Swing	170	Two	C F G Am	4
19	Twinkle, Twinkle, Little Star	Harp	Ballad	126	Two	C F G	4
20	When the Saints Go Marching In	Trumpet	Swing	138	Two	C F G	4